Stalingrad

A Captivating Guide to the Battle of Stalingrad and Its Impact on World War II

Free Bonus from Captivating History
(Available for a Limited time)

Hi History Lovers!

Now you have a chance to join our exclusive history list so you can get your first history ebook for free as well as discounts and a potential to get more history books for free! Simply visit the link below to join.

Captivatinghistory.com/ebook

Also, make sure to follow us on Facebook, Twitter and Youtube by searching for Captivating History.

Contents

Introduction

The Battle of Stalingrad is rightfully known as the "turning point" of the Second World War. Before the battle, which took place from August 1942 until the beginning of February 1943, the Germans were victorious everywhere, despite some localized setbacks (for example, at Moscow in 1941). After Stalingrad, the Germans were constantly pushed back, with some notable examples being Kursk in the summer of 1943 and the Bulge in 1944.

During WWII, the Soviet Union suffered somewhere in the neighborhood of twenty million dead. For those of you reading in the United States and the United Kingdom, the death toll for those nations in the war was around 415,000 and 483,000, respectively. In the approximate six months of the Battle of Stalingrad, the Germans, their Hungarian, Romanian, and Italian allies, and the Soviets lost an estimated one million men.

As the battle wore on, the German soldiers gave the battle in Stalingrad a nickname: "Der Rattenkrieg," or "the war of the rats." The fighting in Stalingrad took place in the ruins of a large city, as well as below in the sewers. Much of the fighting was close-quarter combat, and in many cases, it was hand-to-hand. Men died by the hundreds of thousands, just like dirty, savage rats.

Adolf Hitler originally wanted his 6th Army to protect the northern flank of his armies as they drove into the oil fields and fertile farmlands of the Caucasus, but as time went by, the battle took on a life of its own. In Hitler's mind, the city that bore Stalin's name became a symbol of Soviet resistance and of the Soviet leader himself. If the Germans took the city, perhaps the Soviet Union (USSR) would finally fall, taking Stalin down with it.

Timeline

July 31st, 1942: Hitler orders his troops to move on Stalingrad.

August 23rd-25th: Initial heavy bombing of the city.

August 24th: North of the city, German troops reach the Volga River. In surveying the city, the commander of the German 14th Panzer Division says that the Germans should not attack the city and set up defensive lines farther westward, as the city is too defensible. He is ignored.

August 25th: Fighting begins in the city itself.

September 13th-25th: The city is divided. The Germans are in the north and south, and the Soviets are in the middle. They will gradually be pushed back to an area about 200 meters (around 655 feet) from the Volga, except for a few pockets of resistance, such as Pavlov's House and the factories.

Between September to November: There are 700 organized large-scale German attacks on and in the city.

Late September: General Franz Halder, chief of staff of the German High Command, expresses doubt to Hitler about the ability of the Germans to win at Stalingrad. He voices concerns about Soviet strength, long supply lines, dwindling German manpower reserves, and the weakness of the German allies on the wings of the Stalingrad front. Hitler removes him from command, and he is forcibly retired.

October 7th: Germans occupy much, but not all, of the Tractor Factory complex. The Soviet 62nd Army under Vasily Chuikov is down to approximately 700 men and are pushed back within meters of the Volga. Ninety percent of the city is in German hands. Despite this, Soviet intelligence reports indicate German morale is low and their physical condition poor, while Soviet morale seems to be growing, sparked by the determined defense of the city.

November 11th: The last major German push fails to take the city.

November 13th: Stalin approves Operation Uranus.

On November 3rd, German soldier Wilhelm Hoffman wrote in his diary, "In the last few days, our battalion has several times tried to attack the Russian positions—to no avail. On this sector, the Russians won't let you lift your head. There have been a number of cases of self-inflicted wounds and malingering among the men."

On November 10th, while the Russians were planning a big surprise attack, Hoffman wrote, "A letter from Elsa today. Everyone expects us home for Christmas. In Germany everyone believes we already hold Stalingrad. How wrong they are. If they could only see what Stalingrad has done to our army."

Illustration 1: German veteran well into the campaign

Chapter 1 – Before the Battle

Hitler's armies invaded the USSR on June 22nd, 1941, setting off Operation Barbarossa. Three million men, more than three thousand tanks, and thousands of combat aircraft surged across the Soviet border within days, and the Germans pushed the Soviet Red Army back a hundred miles or more. The attack came as a total shock to Josef Stalin, the Soviet leader, despite the many warnings he had received from his military officials, diplomats, and spies.

Germany and the Soviet Union had signed a non-aggression pact, known as the Molotov-Ribbentrop Pact, in August 1939. This pact divided Poland between them, gave Stalin the green light to annex the Baltic states without German interference, and allowed Stalin to make demands on Finland without having to worry about Hitler. Both sides benefited from the pact in other ways as well. Germany would buy huge amounts of Soviet raw materials and food; in return, the Germans would not have to worry about a Soviet conflict when it turned to attack Western Europe. The Soviets, on the other hand, would get hard currency, German machinery, factory parts, and other highly refined goods.

Stalin believed that Hitler would eventually attack the Soviet Union, but he believed that it would be stalled by the pact and perhaps prevented entirely by further negotiations. The terms of the pact were, in theory, to last ten years, which, in Stalin's mind, would give him the time he needed to finalize the massive efforts to modernize the USSR, which he had begun in the early 1930s.

Additionally, Stalin believed what Hitler had written in his book, *Mein Kampf*. Hitler thought the reason why Germany was defeated in World War One was the fact that it had undertaken a two-front war, one against France and Britain in the West and one against Russia in the East. Other parts of Hitler's book emphasized the need for Germany to expand into what Hitler considered "the empty spaces of Russia." Stalin would have done well to place his emphasis on that and Hitler's irrationality when it came to Russia and communism than on the idea that Hitler would not engage in two fronts at once.

By the end of June 1940, Hitler had successfully invaded Poland, Norway, Denmark, Belgium, Holland, and France. Great Britain seemed to be all but defeated; its armies in mainland Europe had been driven back across the English Channel. Hermann Göring, Hitler's second-in-command and chief of the *Luftwaffe* (the German air force), assured Hitler that the British would soon ask for terms of surrender or be defeated outright in the invasion that the German armed forces had been planning.

In the winter of 1939/40, Stalin ordered the Red Army to attack Finland after the Finnish government refused Stalin's demands to hand over a sizable portion of its lands bordering the USSR. Though Stalin's forces eventually prevailed, with Finland forced to give the land to the Soviet Union, the performance of the Red Army in the conflict was largely poor. Hitler, along with most of the world, saw this inferior performance and determined that the Red Army was no match for his victorious armed forces (known in German as the *Wehrmacht*).

The German High Command had been ordered to plan for an invasion of the USSR shortly after the defeat of France in June 1940. Over the following months, the Germans perfected their plan, which

Hitler wanted to take place in May 1941. However, some of his generals were pessimistic about the proposed operation; they believed the USSR was too large and too strong to be defeated, especially while Great Britain was still in the fight. They reminded Hitler of the dangers of fighting a two-front war, something that he himself had blamed for Germany's defeat in WWI.

Other members of the German General Staff had been cautious and reserved about the idea of invading the Soviet Union, but they became more enthusiastic after the rapid defeat of France and the seemingly poor performance of the Red Army in the Winter War against Finland. A small number were keen on the idea of an invasion from the start, believing, like Hitler, that the USSR would fold as easily as France and the rest of Europe.

This is often seen as one of the top ten greatest military blunders in all of history. But in the first few weeks of Operation Barbarossa (which began in late June 1941), it seemed that Hitler might be right. Huge numbers of Soviet prisoners were taken from the battles on the plains and rolling hills of western Russia. Aside from the hundreds of thousands of Soviet prisoners taken, hundreds of thousands more were killed. The *Wehrmacht* drove hundreds of miles into eastern Poland, which had been under Stalin's control since the Molotov-Ribbentrop Pact of 1939, and the Soviet Union.

Though the German blitzkrieg ("lightning war") tactics completely flummoxed the defending Soviets, the Red Army did not help their own cause, as they played right into German hands. The blitzkrieg depended on highly coordinated attacks between air, ground (both armored and infantry), and artillery forces, trying as best as they could to bring overwhelming force to bear on weak points of the Soviet lines. Once they had punched a hole in the lines, the armored and mechanized infantry would pour through, moving swiftly to the enemy's rear to surround them, with the bulk of the regular infantry attacking the front lines at the same time to hold the enemy in place.

Instead of coordinating their attacks properly, the Soviets attacked and counterattacked everywhere, regardless of whether it was strategically or tactically sound. The reason for this had to do with the nature of the Stalinist regime and Stalin's reaction to Hitler's invasion. In the late 1930s, Josef Stalin had carried out a purge of the Red Army, seeing enemies everywhere. He had done the same shortly before with the Communist Party of the Soviet Union and much of Soviet society. His paranoia and desire for total control resulted in perhaps the most totalitarian system in history.

Once Stalin had established his unquestioned control of the country, he was free to attack the Red Army, the one institution that might pose a threat to him. No real evidence exists that anyone in the Red Army was plotting against him, but to Stalin, a disapproving glance or an unwanted association was enough to get you in trouble.

In 1937, Stalin's secret police began a purge of the officer ranks of the army, decimating the higher ranks and arresting thousands of lower-ranking officers. Thousands of men were killed outright. Many more were sent to Siberia, where most of them perished in the labor camp system known as the Gulag. Those on the secret police's lists who weren't arrested were forced into retirement. Stalin was then left with an army that would not dare to defy or question any of Stalin's edicts, orders, or "suggestions." This was one reason for the poor showing of the Red Army against Finland in 1939/40.

The Finnish debacle had shown to Stalin that the Soviets' use of mass infantry attacks was a poor method to use in modern warfare, and reforms were slowly being instituted. However, by June 22nd, 1941, the opening date of Operation Barbarossa, these had not filtered down to most of the army.

Aside from the institutional problems, Stalin's reaction to Hitler's attack was a combination of disbelief, panic, and depression. Initially, the "Great Leader" refused to believe that Hitler's forces were actually attacking. Then, when confronted with the proof, Stalin ordered virtually every unit facing the Germans to attack, regardless of their situation. This meant that unorganized, retreating, or surrounded units haphazardly attacked with virtually no preparation. To them, it was better to take a chance on the battlefield than the sure bullet in the back, as Stalin's secret police were seemingly everywhere (including with commanders at the front).

After giving vague orders to "attack," Stalin retreated to his vacation retreat, or *dacha*, in the forest, which was miles from Moscow. When a group of officials, including his trusted Foreign Minister Vyacheslav Molotov, appeared at his home, Stalin appeared "strange and downcast," not like his regular self. Stalin thought they had come to arrest him, for when Molotov told Stalin that they thought a central committee tasked with the war effort should be formed immediately, Stalin asked, "Who is to head this committee?" When Molotov replied, "You," Stalin knew he was safe and began to break through his depression. Still, despite Stalin's "reawakening," the Soviets continued to be pushed back.

However, by the early fall, the Red Army's defense had begun to stiffen. Though defeated in huge battles around Smolensk and Vyazma, among other places, the Germans found that the farther they drove toward the Soviet capital of Moscow and the Soviet "second city" of Leningrad, the stiffer Soviet resistance became.

The Nazis also had some rude shocks in the first weeks of the invasion. Though the Red Army was losing men in droves (with men either killed in action or taken prisoner), there always seemed to be more of them. Additionally, the Germans found out that their tanks were inferior to the newest Soviet tanks, the famed T-34 and KV-1. However, these tanks were just entering production when the war began, so their numbers were low. The Soviets also did not know how to use them properly, throwing them into action haphazardly and in badly coordinated attacks.

Lastly, the geography of the USSR began to slowly take a toll on the Germans. The country consists of hundreds upon hundreds of miles of plains, with nary a tree as a landmark. It was a land that was completely foreign to the invading forces. And although it is commonly thought that the German Army was a highly mechanized force, this was not the case. Most infantrymen marched, and most of their supplies came on horse-drawn wagons. This was detrimental to the German war effort in the USSR, as the country had poor roads and primitive (and differently sized) railway systems.

While the Russian winter is well known for its harshness, the summers on the plains can be brutal as well. There is no shade, barely any water (especially since the retreating Soviets had poisoned many wells), dust, and endless marches before the terror of combat. After a time, German morale began to suffer. This happened slowly at first, as they had some tremendous victories to help encourage them, but as the weeks passed, discontent grew. Their one final victory always seemed to be just out of reach, despite predictions of the war ending soon from the Nazi Party and the Führer.

At the beginning of September 1941, the Germans were at the gates of Leningrad, but they were not able to enter the city. The Red Army, as well as Leningrad's civilians, had prepared a belt of defenses that were just too strong for the Germans to easily break. Instead, the Nazis ringed the city and began an almost 900-day siege, which claimed over one million lives, most of them civilians.

In the south of the country, the Germans, along with their Hungarian, Italian, and Romanian allies, drove deep into Ukraine, besieging Odessa (spelled as Odesa today) and pushing out to the shores of the Black Sea and the Crimean Peninsula.

In the middle of the German drive, their Army Group Center, led by Field Marshal Fedor von Bock, found itself at the gates of Moscow at the beginning of December. Some units reported seeing the domes of St. Basil's Cathedral in the Kremlin glinting in the sun far in the distance. That is as close as they would ever get.

Even with the seemingly endless supply of men the Germans were facing, the Soviets had more men fighting in the Soviet Far East. They were there to guard against a possible Japanese attack, as the Soviets suspected the Japanese would seize the resources of Siberia, but Soviet spies and diplomats informed Stalin that the Japanese had other plans. Stalin, in desperate need and now more believing of his intelligence services, ordered the transfer of hundreds of thousands of men to attack the Germans at Moscow, which they did on December 5th, 1941, driving the Germans back over one hundred miles before being halted.

By late January 1942, the front lines in Russia had stabilized, and Hitler began to plan for a spring/summer offensive as soon as the weather permitted.

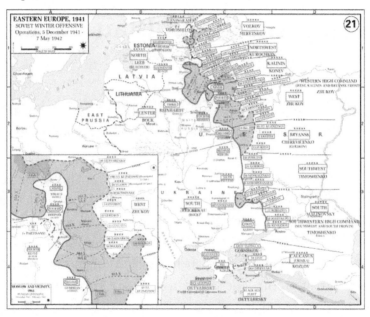

Illustration 2: General front lines after Soviet Moscow offensive until the spring of 1942

Chapter 2 – Fall Blau ("Case Blue")

Fall Blau was the operational name for Hitler's planned attack into southern Russia, which included the Caucasus Peninsula, home to some of the world's most productive oil fields at the time.

The Germans needed oil more than almost any other natural resource. Without it, there was no realistic way for them to win the war. Germany itself produced next to none, and the Romanian fields in and around Ploesti were not enough to keep the German war machine rolling. Tanks, planes, U-boats, and other support vehicles were dependent on oil. The Germans had stockpiled large quantities before the war, but that had essentially vanished. They were using more than they could produce or import, especially considering the lock the British Royal Navy had on the oceanic trade routes.

Hitler was confronted with a serious dilemma at the start of spring in 1942. He was no longer strong enough to attack on all fronts as he had been in 1941, and the Soviets (to his surprise) were not defeated. So, to knock the Soviets out of the war, which would allow Hitler to concentrate on the final defeat of the United Kingdom and the United

States (with whom he declared war on December 11th, 1941), he and the German General Staff had to come up with a plan.

A considerable number of German generals encouraged Hitler not to go on the offensive at all. They argued that it was best for Germany to build up its defenses where they stood or perhaps even pull back to a more defensible position. They also argued that not only were the German oil reserves being depleted at a rapid rate, but the number of combat-age men was going to start declining very soon. Additionally, the *Luftwaffe*, which was still controlling the skies above the battlefield, was barely making up for its losses and losing skilled pilots almost daily.

Some also argued that the German push in North Africa, which had the stated goal of seizing the Suez Canal (thereby adding thousands of U-boat-infested miles to British ships coming from the Middle East and India with supplies) and potentially gaining control of the oil fields of Arabia, might be reinforced with men from Russia should the Führer decide to establish defensible lines on the Eastern Front.

As you likely know, Hitler would have none of this. He was convinced that the Germans were just one strong push away before the Soviets either collapsed or begged for peace. Once this was done, Hitler would establish his eastern empire along the Ural Mountains and Volga River. Beyond that expanse of territory, at least in his mind, was nothing but empty space, where the surviving Russians would go to freeze and starve to death.

The force responsible for carrying out Case Blue was Army Group South. This army group was originally commanded by Field Marshal Fedor von Bock, but he was replaced with Field Marshal Maximilian von Weichs in July, as Hitler believed Bock had not carried out his plans rapidly enough. To fulfill Hitler's plan, Army Group South was split into two groups: Army Group A and Army Group B.

Army Group A, commanded by Field Marshal Wilhelm List, was tasked with taking the Caucasus and its oil fields, most of which were in the city of Baku, far to the southeast. It consisted of the German 1ˢᵗ Panzer Army, the 11ᵗʰ Army, the 17ᵗʰ Army, and the 3ʳᵈ Romanian Army.

Army Group B was originally given the task of protecting Army Group A's flank and cutting off the trade and access to resources on the Volga River at Stalingrad. This army group was composed of the German 4ᵗʰ Panzer Army, the 2ⁿᵈ Army, and the 6ᵗʰ Army, which was Hitler's largest army. The Italian 8ᵗʰ, the Romanian 4ᵗʰ, and the Hungarian 2ⁿᵈ Armies were also attached. Army Group B was commanded by Weichs after Army Group South was divided.

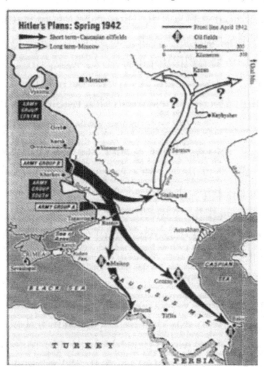

Illustration 3: The basic plan for Case Blue, spring 1942

Over the course of time, the main goal of the German thrust changed from the oil fields to Stalingrad. By the time the battle actually began in the city, Stalingrad seemed to be like a giant malevolent black hole, drawing men to their deaths.

Although the Caucasus was supposed to be the main objective, the stronger and more numerous 6th Army approached Stalingrad right from the get-go. The 6th Army had never seen defeat. The men of the 6th Army had paved the way in the West, playing a central role in the defeat of Belgium and France and driving the British Expeditionary Force from the mainland. In the initial stages of Operation Barbarossa, they had driven the Red Army back and inflicted decisive defeats at the Battle of Uman (mid-July to early August 1941) and taken Kiev (late August to late September), one of the Soviet Union's most important and historic cities. The 6th Army had done the same to the important Ukrainian city of Kharkov during a swift and fierce battle in late October. The German force repulsed a strong Soviet counterattack there in May 1942, just before it began its drive toward the Volga.

So, as the 6th Army moved on Stalingrad, morale was high, despite its relatively unknown and taciturn commander, General Friedrich Paulus. Paulus became the commander of the 6th Army in January 1942, taking it over from the more experienced and highly popular commander Field Marshal Walther von Reichenau. Reichenau had moved up to command Army Group South in November, and for two months, the 6th Army did not have a commander. When Paulus was named its chief, many in the 6th Army, and the German Army in general, were surprised, for Paulus had never commanded a unit larger than a battalion in combat. Two months after Paulus took command of the 6th Army, Reichenau died of natural causes, which greatly affected the men and left Paulus without someone familiar with the position to consult with.

As a side note, many WWII histories, especially from before the 1990s, write Paulus's name as "von Paulus." "Von" signifies nobility, which Paulus was not. It was also sometimes given to men by Germany's leaders as a sign of respect and recognition. Hitler never bestowed this honor on Paulus. Historians sometimes assume that because he was made a field marshal, he was given the "von" title as well, but he was not.

Paulus was a highly regarded planner and showed sound strategic instinct. Like virtually all of the German general officers, Paulus had spent considerable time on the German General Staff, which was responsible for most of the planning for the German Army's campaigns (of course, Hitler played an increasingly large part as the war went on). Paulus had been deputy chief of the General Staff after leading troops in campaigns in Poland and the West. In that position, he played a large part in the planning of Operation Barbarossa. Paulus was no stranger to war in the East, but in an army that was increasingly becoming known worldwide for its dashing and unorthodox thinkers (such as Rommel and Guderian, to name just two), Paulus was regarded as relatively unimaginative and uninspiring. He also did not cut a very dashing figure. He was small and slightly haggard-looking; he looked more like a head waiter than a general leading one of the world's most powerful fighting forces into combat.

Still, Paulus was a sound planner, and he was considered to be an expert logician, as he understood the supply chain and how to get men, equipment, and supplies where they needed to be when they needed to be there.

So, all things considered, the men of the 6th were in high spirits when Case Blue began. Aside from their record in combat, the 6th had great numbers of the German Army's most modern equipment, as well as the support of the powerful air forces.

At the beginning of Case Blue, the Axis forces (including the 6th Army, the 4th Panzer Army, and other German forces and assorted allied forces) had 1.5 million men, almost 2,000 tanks and assault guns, and an estimated 1,600 to 2,100 aircraft. To put this in perspective (at least in terms of numbers), in 2020, the entire US Army is expected to include just over a million personnel and just over 2,000 fighter aircraft.[1] As one can see, the German forces driving deep into the southern Soviet Union were formidable.

However, they did have a number of weaknesses, the prime of which was supply. Not only were the German supply lines now about 1,000 miles in length, but much of that supply came to the 6th Army and arrived via horse-drawn wagons. The transport of supplies was also slowed by the railways of the Soviet Union, as they were of a smaller gauge (width) than the rest of Europe. As a result, cargo had to be transferred. Soviet partisans were also growing in strength and organization, and they increasingly interrupted the flow of supplies to all the German forces in the USSR.

In addition to food and ammunition, this meant that replacements had to travel an exceptional distance, as well as replacement parts and fuel. As the campaign wore on, and the weather turned, supply logistics became one of the largest problems facing the Germans at Stalingrad.

Making matters even worse for the Germans was a complete intelligence lapse regarding Soviet strength. They had underestimated Stalin's power in 1941, but due to the factors mentioned above, they were able to defeat the Red Army in battle after battle. At the Battle of Moscow, which began in September 1941, the Germans believed the Soviets were on their last legs—and then the Red Army attacked with a fresh force of over 250,000 men. This happened over and over during the war with the USSR.

In the spring of 1942, German intelligence estimated the total Soviet aircraft to be just over 6,500. The reality (and this does include some obsolete and non-combat aircraft) was that the Soviets had over 20,000. The Germans also believed the Soviets were roughly on par with them in terms of tanks, which was around 6,000. Again, the reality was far different: it was nearly 25,000 on all fronts. Lastly,

---

1.   Globalfirepower.com.

Soviet artillery was far stronger than the Germans believed, as they thought the Reds possessed nearly 8,000 guns. The Soviets actually possessed more than 30,000. (Artillery was produced in unbelievable quantities in the USSR during the war. At the Battle of Berlin in 1945, it's estimated that the Soviets had a gun placed every ten yards around the city, accounting for lapses of geography and tactics; this number does not include mortars and the famed "Katyusha" rocket launchers.)

In June 1942, Hitler met with Finnish Marshal Carl Gustaf Emil Mannerheim, his ally, on the Finn's seventy-fifth birthday in an attempt to coax him to move Finnish forces deeper into the Soviet Union, which Mannerheim refused to do. Part of their conversation was recorded by a Finnish broadcast technician. In the conversation, Hitler admits the Germans grossly underestimated Soviet strength.

"It is evident...evident. They have the most monstrous armament that is humanly conceivable...so...if anybody had told me that one state...if anybody had told me that one state can line up with 35,000 tanks, I had said 'you have gone mad.'"

The totals mentioned above represented the Soviet strength along the entire Eastern Front in the spring of 1942. Just a portion of their power faced German Army Groups A and B during the planned German spring offensive.

While the Soviet Union's strength was immense and growing enormously by the week, the Red Army had sustained unbelievable losses in the first year of the war, and though the Germans had been pushed back or held in place, they were still close to Moscow and just outside Leningrad. The Soviet generals were still hesitant to take the initiative, even though they were slowly being given more leeway to do so by Stalin (who had begun to realize he was not the military genius he believed himself to be). On top of that, thousands of Soviet towns and cities had been destroyed, and much of its most productive agricultural areas were occupied. And, of course, there were the terrible civilian casualties.

As the Germans pushed eastward, the Soviets began to move as much of their still existing productive capacity to the area of the Ural Mountains, beyond the range of the German bombers. In the spring of 1942, many of these factories were literally operating in open fields by generators. But every day, progress was being made, and within a relatively short time, the factories of the Urals were turning out unreal quantities of weapons, ammunition, and other necessities for the war. Historians who focus on logistics and production consider this Soviet effort to be one of the most miraculous of modern times. It was, of course, achieved at a high cost, both in money and in lives.

Focusing back on the southern front, an estimated 1,700,000 Soviets faced the German forces in the spring and summer of 1942, with possibly one million in reserve far to the rear. These men were in various states of formation, organization, training, and outfitting. Along with the soldiers were some 3,000 to 3,800 tanks, over 1,500 aircraft of all types, and over 16,000 guns, mortars, and rocket launchers.

The Red Army, on paper, was formidable, but they were still on the defensive. Making matters worse was another Soviet intelligence blunder. After the Battle of Stalingrad, Soviet military intelligence would improve vastly for a number of reasons, but before the battle, it suffered from a lack of imagination, hesitancy to report bad news to Stalin, and resources.

The Soviets were relatively sure that the Germans would not be able to mount the same broad offensive as Operation Barbarossa; the Nazis had sustained great casualties as well, though not on the level of the Red Army. As such, Stalin's generals were confident they did not have to fear a repeat of that summer.

However, the Soviet General Staff (known by its Russian language acronym, "STAVKA") was in a quandary. One of its most important cities, Leningrad, was under siege. The Soviet capital, while not under immediate threat, was still obviously a potential target, and the Germans were only 150 to 200 miles from Moscow. Losing either of those cities could possibly be catastrophic, and so, the Soviets reinforced both areas strongly.

In war, as in American or even European football, the team that possesses the ball has a distinct advantage, at least at first, as they know where they're going. Defenders, in football and in war, have to make their best guess and commit. If they commit incorrectly, great damage might be done.

And, in the spring of 1942, the Soviets guessed incorrectly. They had spent much of the winter trying to figure out where the Germans would attack when the good weather came. They gathered and sifted through intelligence of all sorts, and they tried to put themselves in the Germans' shoes. The conclusion that STAVKA came to was that the Germans would make an all-out push toward Moscow. The capital had been the target of the last German effort of 1941, and the men of STAVKA believed it would be so again once the weather improved.

Hitler had determined relatively early in 1942 that his main effort would be in the south, and so, his generals and intelligence services did everything they could to convince the Russians that Moscow was the prize.

Those of you familiar with the Anglo-American effort to fool the Germans in the spring of 1944 as to where they might invade Europe will know that the Allies created fake armies, fake documents (that they "accidentally" let the Germans possess), fake commanders (most notably US General George Patton, who was openly displayed making none too subtle speeches about how he was going to defeat the Germans when the invasion happened), fake radio traffic in codes they knew the Germans had broken, and much more.

The German effort in 1942 was similar, if not as large and detailed. Radio messages were sent in the clear or in codes they knew the Soviets had broken. Suspected Soviet spies were given fake information. Documents were "carelessly" left on the battlefield, and troop movements were simulated along the Moscow front, along with recordings of tank and trucks being played over loudspeakers.

As a result, the Soviets moved significant numbers of troops to the area around Moscow, where the Germans had actually dug in, strengthening their defensive positions. A large portion of the Soviets' industrial production was sent to the Moscow area, and the focus of the Soviet General Staff was the capital. When the German attack began on May 7th, Stalin and his commanders believed it was a feint to lure the Red Army away from Moscow. They were not going to "bite," although they probably should have.

Chapter 3 – The slaughter Begins

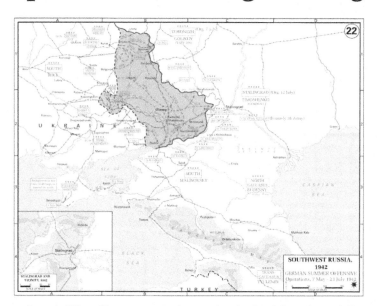

Illustration 4: The German starting point is the blue dotted line. The pink area is what was seized from the Soviets by late July 1942.

Just before Case Blue was to begin, the Soviets began their own attack, which was designed to delay and disrupt what they believed were Germany's intentions toward Moscow. Many of his generals, who were now allowed to express opinions to a certain degree without fear of being arrested, argued that Stalin was mistaken in his idea that the

Germans would be able to launch major attacks on two main fronts. However, Stalin forged ahead and ordered his forces to launch an attack in the area of the Ukrainian cities of Kharkov (today known better by its Ukrainian spelling "Kharkiv") and Izyum. The attack began on May 12th, 1942.

This attack was launched directly into the area where the Germans were building up forces for the upcoming Case Blue. The Soviet offensive took place on a front of some 50 miles and included over 700,000 men and 1,000 tanks of various types. The German forces in the area numbered some 350,000 men with about 500 tanks and nearly 600 aircraft. Soviet air forces in the area outnumbered the German, but at this point in the war, and nearly to its end, German pilots demonstrated considerably greater skill and effectiveness than their Soviet counterparts.

The attack initially took the Germans by surprise, but they fell back in good order, and their forces on the northern and southern ends of the Soviet push held. The Germans retreated in the center as well, which created a massive bulge in the lines, as you can see below.

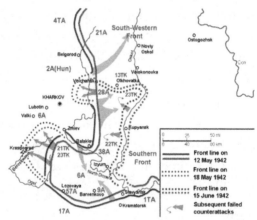

Illustration 5: The Second Battle of Kharkov/Izyum pocket, May/June 1942

This bulge allowed the Germans to do what they had been doing for the entire war, in both the East and the West: out-plan, out-think, and outmaneuver their enemy. On May 17th and 18th, the Germans began their counterattack, which went off in textbook fashion, with excellent coordination between the infantry, armor, artillery, and air forces.

One of the Soviet political officers and Stalin's personal observers in the area was a man named Nikita Khrushchev, who would later become the premier of the Soviet Union in the mid-1950s. Despite local Soviet commanders pleading for permission to retreat to avoid being encircled by the Nazis, Khrushchev and the overall commander of the Red Army offensive, Marshal Semyon Timoshenko, told Stalin that the situation could be contained and that the Germans could be defeated. These men could not have been more wrong. When the upcoming Battle of Stalingrad began, in which Khrushchev was made the highest-ranking political officer in the city, he made sure that he carried out every order received by Stalin to a "T," doing so with murderous zeal, partly to save his own neck.

In the end, the Soviet offensive ended in catastrophe. Almost 300,000 men were killed, wounded, or captured, and over 1,000 tanks were destroyed, along with an equal number of aircraft and huge numbers of guns. Not only were the losses high, but the German offensive shattered the morale of the Soviet forces in the area, who began a disorderly and panicked retreat.

The German commander on the northern shoulder of the bulge near Kharkov was General Paulus, who had been busy planning the upcoming German offensive. The German response gave Paulus the opportunity to lead his men in battle and find out what his new command was capable of.

Case Blue Begins

On June 28th, 1942, two weeks after the Soviet attack had been contained and repulsed, the Germans began *Fall Blau*.

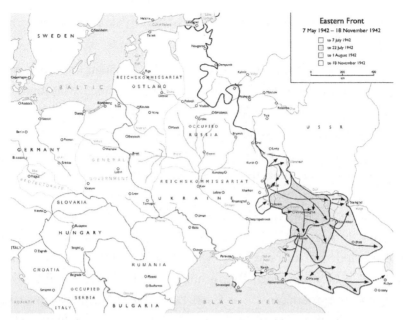

Illustration 6: German attacks from July to November 1942. Map courtesy of User: Gdr – based on: Overy, Richard (2019) World War II Map by Map, DK, pp. 148-150 ISBN: 9780241358719., CC BY-SA 3.0 wikipedia commons

One of the foot soldiers taking part in the German offensive was Wilhelm Hoffman of the 267th Infantry Regiment of the 94th Infantry Division, 6th Army. Hoffman is remembered for his personal diary, which was discovered after the war. It is one of the few surviving memoirs of the personal experiences of a German soldier as the Battle of Stalingrad happened. Hoffman was killed shortly after Christmas 1942—his personal effects, including his diary, were sent home.

His diary starts off cheerily, reflecting the high morale of the Germans as they began their drive to defeat the Soviets. In the words of Hoffman, "take Stalingrad, and then the war will be over for us." On July 29th, Hoffman wrote, "the company commander says that the Russian troops are completely broken and cannot hold out much longer. To reach the Volga and take Stalingrad is not so difficult for us. The Führer knows where the Russians' weak point is. Victory is not far away."

And it appeared that way to many in the German 6th Army. Well, perhaps not to some of the more grizzled veterans, who had been fighting since the previous year's invasion. They, too, had been told that it was likely only a matter of months, maybe even weeks, before the Soviets gave in. These veterans knew that two of the most important German objectives, Leningrad and Moscow, were still in Soviet hands, and although the Soviets lost millions, they seemed to keep putting fresh men into the field. And though the Red Army had been mostly retreating, their defense was getting more stubborn and more skilled by the day. At Sebastopol in Crimea, the Soviets withstood a German siege for months, and though it would fall just before the commencement of Case Blue, the Russian defense there had been fanatical. There was even an incident in which political commissars and other officers detonated charges in the underground ammunition caverns, where they and hundreds of civilians and soldiers were holed up. These detonations killed virtually everyone, but the Soviets would rather have this happen than be taken as prisoners. All of this gave the German veterans pause, but still, they had had the Soviets on the run for most of the last year.

On August 2nd, Hoffman wrote, "What great spaces the Soviets occupy, what rich fields are to be had here after the war's over! ... I believe that the Führer will carry the thing through to a successful end." On August 10th, he wrote, "The Führer's orders were read out to us. He expects victory of us. We are all convinced that they can't stop us."

As the Germans advanced, sometimes forty or more miles in a day, Hitler's confidence rose. On July 17th, the Germans were victorious in a large battle on the Chir River near Kalach, about ninety miles from Stalingrad. This victory reinforced Hitler's belief that the Soviets were nearly finished, and he made what some believe to be a fatal error (the first of many at Stalingrad): he took apart his weakened but still considerable 11th Army and sent parts of it north to help in the siege of Leningrad. In hindsight, these forces could have been used more effectively and perhaps more decisively at Stalingrad.

As the Germans advanced, the Red Army gave way before them, retreating over the wide Don River where it bends to the south and at its closest point to Stalingrad and the Volga. The retreat away from the Don River meant that the Soviets had no natural obstacles behind which to set up a strong defense. The next truly defensible position was Stalingrad itself. If the Soviets retreated across to the eastern side of the Volga, the war might end, as the Germans would cut off one of the USSR's main lifelines and be free to move south into the Caucasus without fear of an attack on their northern flank.

Order #227

That being the case, Josef Stalin issued a directive: "Order #227," sometimes known as the "Not one step back" order. The directive itself was never published and distributed publicly. Stalin did read it over the airwaves, and his subordinates were very aware of its contents, among which was the establishment of penal battalions for each "front" grouping. (In the Soviet system of command, the "front," such as the newly formed "Bryansk Front" and "Voronezh Front" in the area near Stalingrad, were equivalent to the Germany "Army Group.") These penal battalions would be made up of men who were deemed to have been shirking their duty, irresponsible, or had committed crimes. The penal battalions, for the most part, were a death sentence, as these men carried out the most dangerous assignments (like defusing mines under German fire), though Stalin did give these men "an opportunity to redeem by blood their crimes against the Motherland."

Order #227 also established "blocking detachments," which would be made up of men from the secret police. These units were empowered to shoot men retreating without orders or round them up to send to the penal battalions.

The order also authorized the immediate arrest of any officer—of any grade—who either ordered unauthorized retreats or accepted the retreat of their units without orders. Most of these men were taken away and shot, though some did end up in the penal battalions, where the majority died.

In the first three months of the battle in Stalingrad, blocking detachments shot an estimated 1,000 men and sent almost 25,000 to penal battalions. By October, the front lines had begun to stabilize, and the blocking detachments were slowly phased out, though they remained a part of the Soviet armed forces until 1944.

Stalin rewrote the order himself after his generals had come up with a very sterile document without any real patriotic feeling. Here are some examples:

"Some stupid people at the front calm themselves with talk that we can retreat further to the east, as we have a lot of territory, a lot of ground, a lot of population and that there will always be much bread for us. They want to justify the infamous behavior at the front. But such talk is a falsehood, helpful only to our enemies."

"Therefore it is necessary to eliminate talk that we have the capability endlessly to retreat, that we have a lot of territory, that our country is great and rich, that there is a large population, and that bread always will be abundant. Such talk is false and parasitic, it weakens us and benefits the enemy, if we do not stop retreating we will be without bread, without fuel, without metal, without raw material, without factories and plants, without railways. This leads to the conclusion, it is time to finish retreating. Not one step back! Such should now be our main slogan."

Historians argue the effect of the order, saying that by the time of the Battle of Stalingrad, it was apparent to almost everyone that retreat was not an option and that losing the city could possibly lead to losing oil, the Volga, and the war. Others argue the order was necessary after all the defeats in the south, as well as the considerable setbacks elsewhere since the beginning of the war. They believe harsh discipline was needed to stop a panic.

Later in the battle, and in the war, the Germans adopted the use of blocking units and summary execution. Penal battalions had been a fact of life in the German Army for some time.

August 23rd, 1942

The *Luftwaffe* launched nearly 2,000 sorties over Stalingrad (a "sortie" is an individual flight—if a plane flew five sorties, it flew five times), employing medium and dive bombers. Many of the bombs that dropped on Stalingrad were incendiary, and in addition to the explosions of these and other ordnances, much of the city was destroyed in one day.

The smoke from the city rose two miles into the air and could be seen miles away. It was a devastating attack. Stalingrad's pre-war population was about 850,000 to 900,000. The numbers of dead given for the bombing raid, which lasted from August 23rd to August 25th, range from about 900 to over 40,000. After comparing similar raids on similar-sized cities throughout the war and examining Soviet documents after the fall of the Soviet Union, most researchers put the total between 10,000 to 15,000 people.

When the Germans finished bombing, Stalingrad was essentially "gone." Most of its largest buildings were now mere shells filled with rubble. The streets likewise disappeared, filled with debris from fallen buildings. The poorer civilian areas on the outskirts of the city and in its southern parts, which was mostly composed of wood, were gone. Some buildings did remain, but they were few and heavily damaged.

Stalingrad's downtown, which was considered to be beautiful by many before the war, was demolished. Some of its factories sustained great damage, but they managed to keep producing, sometimes without roofs or most of their walls.

The *Luftwaffe* command believed that they had won the battle before it had even properly started, and German soldiers, watching wave after wave of bombers fly over Stalingrad, wondered how anything could survive. Many expected they would just march into the city and take it.

They couldn't have been more wrong, for what the *Luftwaffe* actually did was create fortresses—fortresses of rubble. The collapsed buildings managed to form "highways" through the rubble, and throughout the battle, the Soviets (and later the Germans) created more. The rubble also provided built-in strong points and bunkers. Aerial reconnaissance was made almost useless. The rubble also allowed snipers to disappear within the ruins and repeatedly strike without ever being seen. The Soviets had been training thousands of snipers before the war even began, both men and women, so they were skilled and dangerous.

Famously, despite all of the damage, one of Stalingrad's most recognizable statues, that of a group of small children playing in one of the city's main squares, survived. You can see it below, with a picture of it then and now.

Many people believe that Stalin ordered no civilians to be evacuated from the city before the battle began, with his belief being that his soldiers would fight harder if civilians remained among them. This is not true. Civilian evacuations began the day after the first German bombing. Within the first days, over 100,000 people were sent eastward over the Volga to relative safety. More followed during the first part of the battle, when it could be managed.

However, many refused to go, voluntarily remaining at their factory jobs and helping the army and the medics. Many of those who lived in the city's outskirts fell under German control. Sometimes they were treated decently, sometimes not. Many times, they were just ignored. Within the city, many took to the basements that still existed or lived in factories. Some even made "homes" within the rubble. Still, when the battle was over in February, the civilian population of Stalingrad numbered an estimated 2,000 to 5,000 people, a far cry of what it had held before. The rest were either evacuated or killed.

Illustration 7: Stalingrad in the spring after the battle, 1943

Chapter 4 – Soldiers and Generals

You have already read about German General Friedrich Paulus. Paulus, along with his comrades Field Marshal Erich von Manstein and General Herman Hoth, are the most recognizable names among the Germans at Stalingrad. Of course, for military historians, many other German soldiers are well known, for, though they ultimately lost the battle, the Germans within Stalingrad fought bravely against some harsh odds.

As the Germans pushed toward the city, they faced resistance from a number of Soviet units. Driving into the outskirts and into the downtown area, they were up against two Soviet armies: the 62nd and the 64th. From July to August 1942, General Vasily Chuikov commanded the 64th, and in August, the command was given to General Mikhail Shumilov, who commanded the army through the rest of the battle. Shumilov would fight until the end of the war and receive distinction in various positions.

Up until September 11th, the 62nd Army was commanded by Generals Vladimir Kolpachy (July to August 1942) and Anton Lopatin (August to September 1942). These men were able, and they ended the war as "Heroes of the Soviet Union," but as the battle began to rage within the city, Stalin determined a different kind of commander needed to take charge of the 62nd. This man was the former commander of the 64th Army: Vasily Chuikov.

Illustration 8: Vasily Chuikov before Stalingrad

In the United States, Generals Dwight D. Eisenhower, George S. Patton, and Douglas MacArthur are held up as heroic leaders during WWII. In the United Kingdom, it's Field Marshals Bernard Montgomery and Harold Alexander. In the Soviet Union, Marshal Georgy Zhukov, Marshal Ivan Konev, and General (later Marshal) Vasily Chuikov (with some others) are lionized. These men, through their own performance and the added efforts of the Soviet propaganda machine, were made into almost superhumans, and they are regarded in the same way today.

Chuikov was born in 1900, near Moscow. He died in 1982 and is buried on Mamayev Kurgan, a height overlooking Stalingrad (now Volgograd). It is one of the most famous sites of the Battle of Stalingrad. In addition to being awarded the "Hero of the Soviet

Union" (the USSR's highest honor) twice, Chuikov was also given the Distinguished Service Cross from the United States for his actions at Stalingrad.

In 1917, the year of the Bolshevik Revolution, Chuikov and his brother joined the revolutionary Red Guards. In 1918, he joined the Red Army proper. Though the Red Army was new, and many of its commander quite young, Chuikov, at the age of eighteen, quickly rose to deputy company commander in the Russian Civil War, and the next year, he commanded a regiment in Siberia.

Chuikov was wounded four times during the Russian Civil War. One of these wounds caused his left arm to become partially paralyzed for life, and a fragment remained in it until the end of his days. It actually caused the infection that killed him in 1982. Chuikov was awarded the "Order of the Red Banner" twice for bravery.

In the 1920s, Chuikov, along with many other Soviet officers, served as advisors to the Chinese Army (the Nationalists). There, he led the Soviet forces in a large battle against a powerful local warlord in northern China for control of the Soviet Far Eastern Railway. During the beginning of China's war with Japan in the 1930s, Chuikov was sent again to help the Chinese in their fight against the Japanese and to help ensure the Chinese remained in the war to keep Japan from attacking the USSR.

In 1939, Chuikov commanded the 4th Army in Stalin's invasion of Poland, as well as the 9th Army in the Russo-Finnish War, both with distinction.

As the commander of the 64th Army, Chuikov had forestalled a major German attack, which allowed the 62nd Army to avoid encirclement. Already well known to Stalin for being a skilled and particularly hard-nosed commander, Chuikov was given command of the 62nd Army and what remained of the 1st Tank Army when the fighting erupted in Stalingrad proper.

Right from the start, Chuikov sent a message to his troops. There would be no more retreating. He personally told Stalin's "eyes and ears" in the city, Nikita Khrushchev, that "I'll either keep them [the Germans] out, or die trying." This was meant not only for him but for his officers and men as well. Chuikov knew how dire the situation at Stalingrad was, not only locally but for the war effort in general. To that end, he had a significant number of officers and men executed for cowardice.

At the beginning of the battle, Chuikov saw one of his main tasks as adding "backbone" to the Red Army units under his command. During the latter part of the battle, he was interviewed, in which he said, "To be honest, most of the divisional commanders didn't really want to die in Stalingrad. The second something went wrong, they'd start saying: 'Permit me to cross the Volga.' I would yell 'I'm still here' and send a telegram: 'One step back and I'll shoot you!'"

At one point in the battle, the Soviets controlled a mere 10 percent of the city, and much of that was under Chuikov's command. Nearby oil storage facilities were above and around his command bunker. At some point, one or more of these was set alight, and flaming oil poured down the hill into the Soviet trenches and bunkers. Chuikov dutifully and courageously remained in his command bunker, not knowing whether he was about to be roasted alive. The flames burned directly above his HQ.

Chuikov is credited with developing the tactic that may have kept the Soviets from losing the battle. Known as "hugging the enemy," he ordered his men to use the buildings, rubble, sewer tunnels, and newly dug trenches to stay as close to the enemy as possible. This was done to mitigate the German advantage (in the first part of the battle, at least) in tanks, guns, and planes. Coming so close to the Germans meant that the Nazis were frequently unable to bring their heavier weapons to bear for fear of hitting their own men. Stalingrad became an exceptionally brutal battle as a result of this, and the casualties were astronomical.

One of Chuikov's main tasks was to keep the crossing at the Volga River open, as he controlled the west bank of the river. This is how reinforcements and supplies were brought into the city and how wounded and civilians were brought out. Due to Chuikov's efforts, the Soviets fed enough reinforcements into the city to keep the Germans busy. As one can probably tell, Chuikov is considered to be one of the greatest heroes at Stalingrad.

Soldiers: The German *Landser*

The average German foot soldier on the march toward Stalingrad in the summer of 1942 carried his own weapon, which, most of the time, was the famed Mauser K (for "karbine") .98 (for 1898, the year in which the model was developed). Some non-commissioned officers, lieutenants, captains, and special assault units would have been equipped with what the American GIs called the "Burp Gun," named for the sound it made. This was the Maschinenpistole ("machine pistol" or "submachine gun") 40 (for 1940), or the MP 40. It is sometimes incorrectly referred to as the "Schmeisser," after Hugo Schmeisser, who had developed one of the first German submachine guns in 1918, but the design of the MP 40 did not involve Schmeisser.

The Germans also employed large numbers of heavy and medium machine guns, most famously the MG 42, which sometimes called "Hitler's buzz saw" for the terrifying sound it made. The MG 42 was so effective that versions of it are still in use in many of today's armed forces, particularly in Europe. The smaller MG 34 was equally effective.

The plains of southern Russia are hot in the summer and freezing in the winter. The Germans' uniforms were completely inadequate for the winter, but they faced problems during the summer as well. For the men heading toward Stalingrad, who were mostly doing so on foot, the sun was relentless, and the plains offered very little shade. Not helping was the fact that it was quite hot in the summer. Marching in the sometimes 90°F heat, the *Landser* (the nickname for a German infantryman) carried a wool blanket and groundsheet, his famous (but heavy) "coal scuttle" helmet, and a full ammunition belt. On his back would be a leather rucksack, which held his small shovel. A gas mask would be around his neck or hooked to his belt. As a side note, many German soldiers threw away their gas masks, as the use of gas during WWII was virtually nonexistent—although smoke and other pollutants, especially in the burning, rotten environment of Stalingrad, were often always present. In his hand or strapped elsewhere, he would have a cloth bag, which carried spare socks, underwear, and personal items.

Officers and non-commissioned officers might carry a variety of sidearms and their ammo. As the men approached a battle, grenades would be supplied, but oftentimes, one or two were carried in their belt. A combat knife and a canteen would hang from the ammunition belt. If the soldier was in the engineers, or if he was specially tasked, he might carry an anti-personnel or anti-tank mine, but generally, these and other equipment, like the field kitchen, were carried on horse-drawn wagons or sometimes vehicles. All in all, the *Landser* carried between forty to fifty-five pounds of equipment with him on the march.

Up until late 1943 and early 1944, the German soldier was perhaps the best-prepared and best-trained soldier in the world. Toward the war's end, the amazing numbers of casualties cut short training times and increased the number of men entering the armed forces. These men were often quite young and inexperienced, diminishing the army's effectiveness.

*Illustration 9: Typical equipment and uniform
of a German soldier, 1942/43*

Soldiers: The Soviet "Ivan"

The Soviet soldier was known as "Ivan" by both his enemies and his allies. Even within the Red Army, a soldier whose name was not known to his new company might be briefly called "Ivan" in the same way a US soldier might have been called "Joe." Ivan is the Russian equivalent to "John," and it was the most common name in the USSR and often tops the list of baby names in today's Russia and Ukraine. By the time the war broke out in 1941, the Germans had lived and been indoctrinated with Nazi propaganda for eight years. As a result, they viewed this "Ivan" as someone primitive, a brute who scraped by on the steppes of Russia. "Ivan" was tough, which he had to be, for his own government was his worst enemy in peacetime. Despite the gains made by the Soviet Union in the 1930s, the USSR was still a relatively poor country, and whether you lived in the city as a worker or toiled in the fields, the mines, or any other physical job, you had to be tough.

At the start of the war, hundreds of thousands of Soviets became prisoners of war. Besides being poorly led, outfought, and outmaneuvered, many Red Army men gave up simply because they hated Stalin's regime, which may have been even more repressive than Hitler's. However, most soon realized that being taken prisoner by the Nazis was a death sentence. Escapees told of beatings, mass shootings, starvation, and much more. Civilian refugees fleeing the Nazis told the same stories. This helped to stiffen the resolve of the Red Army.

By the time of Stalingrad and Order #227, most "Ivans" were ready to fight to the death and take as many Germans with them as possible. In the street fights that broke out in Stalingrad, "Ivan" essentially became a human weapon, one that the Germans greatly feared.

The situation for the Soviet soldier depended on a lot. Was he a veteran soldier in an established unit? Was he a veteran in a unit that had been beaten or disbanded? Or was he a new recruit? The answers to these questions often dictated the equipment that one received.

In many books, documentaries, and even in the movie *Enemy at the Gates*, Soviet soldiers were hustled to the front lines without any weapons at all. This was true, and not just at Stalingrad. This had also been the case at Leningrad in the winter of 1941, as well as other places in the first half of the war in the USSR. These recruits, some of them with virtually no training whatsoever, were told to stick close to the man in front of them, who *might* have a weapon, and grab it when he fell. Or they could always take one from a corpse. The average lifespan for the Soviet recruit during the worst days of Stalingrad, which were the months of August, September, and October 1942, was *seven minutes* on the front lines.

The decently outfitted Soviet soldier at Stalingrad could be expected to carry a wool blanket into battle. The blanket would be rolled and draped over the chest and back and tied at the ends. He wore or carried his helmet and sometimes had a garrison hat slipped through his belt. He also wore a rough linen long-sleeved shirt under a quilted jacket. Woolen trousers were worn with the pant legs stuffed into valenki, Russian crushed felt peasant boots, which were great in the winter. Footcloths, not socks, were worn and carried. These were long slips of linen or other cloth wrapped around the foot to the calf under the boots. Many times, Soviet soldiers made do with shoes from home, although they also took them from dead comrades or enemies. Leather boots in the jackboot style (like the Germans) were also worn, especially toward the war's end when supplies were more plentiful.

Heavy wool greatcoats were issued in winter when they were available. The Soviet soldier was generally better prepared for the cold, but he was not impervious to it, especially when he did not have the right equipment. Frostbite was just as much a threat to the Soviets as the Germans.

"Ivan" might carry a number of bags, either tied to his belt or perhaps rolled within his blanket. These might carry a shelter-half (one half of a tent to be paired with that of another soldier), an extra shirt, and other personal items, as well as his canteen, knife, and shovel.

Illustration 10: This modern Russian reenactor wears an accurate Soviet WWII-era uniform and equipment.

"Ivan" carried two main versions of the rugged and accurate Mosin-Nagant rifle during the war, which also made an excellent sniper rifle when equipped with a scope. Only officers wore sidearms; this did not include non-commissioned officers. "Ivan" would carry spare clips for his rifle in his wide pockets or sometimes in an ammunition belt, where he might also slide in a grenade or two (for those familiar with weaponry of WWII, the Soviet grenades resembled the famed German "potato masher").

Another famous symbol of the Soviets in WWII was the PPSh-41 (in Russian, *pistolet-pulemyot Shpagina*—"Shpagin machine pistol"). The PPSh-41, created by Georgy Shpagin, was sometimes called a *papasha* for the sound of its acronym. In Russian, *papasha* means "daddy." The most recognizable version of the machine gun was equipped with a 71-round drum magazine, though by the time the war ended, most of these weapons carried a 35-round box magazine. The weapon was easy to mass-produce, and it was rugged and accurate enough. German soldiers prized the weapon, and they sometimes issued them from captured Soviet stories or tried to take them from enemies on the battlefield.

Below, you can see the MP 40 on the top and the PPSh on the bottom.

During the Battle of Stalingrad, the Germans had real problems with their weapons and vehicles freezing up. The Soviets, on the other hand, did not, for one very clever reason. The oil in vehicles will thicken and freeze in extreme cold, making the vehicle useless. The only remedy for this was to keep the vehicle running all the time, something which, especially for the Germans, cost a lot of fuel. Likewise, guns, from the smallest to the largest cannons, needed to be oiled to work smoothly. The Germans frequently found their weapons and guns frozen solid and useless. The Soviets would add small amounts of gasoline to the oil of vehicles and weapons, which kept them from freezing. This small trick might have saved hundreds of Soviet lives and ruined hundreds of German ones.

Chapter 5 – Schlacht an der Wolga

In German, the word for struggle, battle, or fight is *Kampf*. Sometimes, however, you will see the word *Schlacht* referring to a battle. *Schlacht* means "slaughter," and you will hardly ever see Stalingrad referred to as anything else in that language. It wasn't really a fight or a battle, but it can definitely be considered a slaughter, and not just because the Germans lost. Stalingrad was a place of slaughter. In the space of about six months, nearly a million people died, and another million were wounded or missing.

In even the most graphic of war movies, one cannot get the sense of what fighting or living in Stalingrad was like. Even in relatively realistic movies, like the German *Stalingrad* (1993) or *Enemy at the Gates* (2001), one cannot see, smell, or hear what the men fighting there did.

Because the fighting was so intense virtually all of the time, most of those killed in battle remained where they died or were blown apart. The men left alive had to navigate through streets, alleys, and buildings covered in human organs and limbs. Those wounded in "no man's land" were left in between the two armies, often screaming their lungs out for hours. Neither side was above wounding a man and leaving him somewhere as "bait" for his comrades. This was done with prisoners as well.

Lice were everywhere, and in the winter, swarms of them made directly for the armpits and crotches of the soldiers, where it was warm. They made the soldiers miserable and helped to spread disease.

The population of rats also multiplied. Like many of their fathers had in the trenches and no man's lands of WWI, soldiers had to watch their dead and dying comrades be eaten by rats and sometimes packs of dogs.

Illustration 11: Soviets make their way through the rubble of the city

The fighting in Stalingrad is remembered for a number of things. First, it was the turning point in the war. Unlike so many pivotal points in history, whose importance is sometimes only recognized years afterward, both sides seemed to know that this battle could possibly decide the war. In Catherine Merridale's excellent book about the life of Soviet soldiers during the war, *Ivan's War* (2007), she tells how even the rank and file seemed to know that Stalingrad would be the turning point. One man wrote home, "Without exception, we are all worried about Stalingrad. If the enemy succeeds in taking it, we will all suffer." Another said, "I am writing to you from a historic place at an historic time."

Second, the fighting, to a great degree, was up close and personal. Because Chuikov and other Soviet commanders had told their men to "hug the enemy" and not give an inch of ground, the buildings themselves became miniature battlefields. Sometimes one side would hold one floor, while the other side took the one below, above, or both. The men took to calling this a "layer-cake battle."

The most famous example of such a battle took place at what became known as "Pavlov's House." Today, only a wall of the building stands in Stalingrad (now known as Volgograd), and it is a revered monument.

Illustration 12: The remains and memorial of Pavlov's House today

Illustration 13: Sergeant Yakov Pavlov

Sergeant Yakov Pavlov commanded the platoon that seized the house, and they held it for sixty days. The house held an important position forward of the main Soviet lines, and from it, the "Ivans" inside could see virtually 360 degrees around, as the building was located in an area with wide streets, squares, and avenues. This allowed the men inside to radio Soviet command about German troop movements in the area. They also used runners at times, who had to make their way through the German lines.

Initially, the Germans tried to drive the Soviets out with tanks, but they soon learned that the Panzers were highly vulnerable to attacks from above, where their armor was the thinnest. In early 1941, the Soviets developed a one-man anti-tank rifle, the PTRD-41. This weapon proved ineffective for the most part, but it was effective against lightly armored half-tracks or command vehicles. The rifle, which had a scoped range of 1,000 yards, did prove to be a somewhat useful sniper rifle, although its loud noise and the dust it launched into the air gave the sniper's position away quickly. Against heavier tanks, it was useless—except when fired from above through the thinly roofed turret. This, combined with hundreds of flammable "Molotov cocktails," meant that the German tanks were stopped in their tracks numerous times.

As a result, the Germans had to send infantry attack after infantry attack to capture Pavlov's House. At times, the Germans would be cut down by the score as they approached the house. Other times, they made it inside but only for a while. There, the fighting that made the Battle of Stalingrad so notable took place, as it did over and over again for months. The Germans might take a floor or even two, only to be met with grenades raining down on them from above. Hand-to-hand fighting, a hallmark of Stalingrad, took place regularly, and people fought with sharpened shovels, knives, and picks.

At times during the sixty days, reinforcements would be sent in. Sometimes they would be sent back, with the remaining men from Pavlov's unit telling them they would not leave unless it was in a bag. Still, attrition did take its toll, and more men were sent in. When it was possible, men would sneak through the ruins at night, bringing ammunition, weapons, food, and water. Of course, many men did not make it.

After two months of fighting, the main Soviet lines were able to move forward and relieve Pavlov's men. Sergeant Pavlov and many of the defenders were awarded multiple times for their defense of the building. Pavlov himself became a deputy to the Supreme Soviet of the Russian Republic; he died in 1981. (For you gamers out there, the original *Call of Duty* featured some sites from the Eastern Front. One of the maps is "Pavlov's House.")

The third reason the Battle of Stalingrad is so well remembered today is the snipers that fought there. Of course, the most famous sniper in Stalingrad was Vasily Zaitsev, whose story was told in William Gates's book, *Enemy at the Gates* (1974), and in the 2001 movie of the same name.

Zaitsev's story became so monumental that it is hard to discern what is fact and what is fiction. According to the official line, Zaitsev's kills mounted daily and were promoted in Soviet propaganda. Between his kills and those of the many other Soviet snipers in the city, the Germans were losing an amazing number of officers and signalmen. What is not talked about as much is that the Germans had an extraordinary number of snipers in the city as well, some of them very good. However, the story that has been passed down through time is that Major Erwin König, the head of a "German sniper school," was sent to Stalingrad. His sole purpose was to hunt down and kill Zaitsev. According to the official Soviet story, and Zaitsev himself, after days of pursuing his target, the German was killed by Zaitsev after he spotted the glint of König's scope under a pile of rubble. The only problem is this never happened.

But what did happen? Zaitsev, a shepherd's son from the Ural Mountains who protected his flock by shooting wolves, did, in fact, kill 225 German soldiers in Stalingrad, plus almost a dozen more before the battle. However, because the Soviets knew that Stalingrad might be the pivotal battle of the war, they set about embellishing Zaitsev's story. He became the Soviet "everyman." After all, Zaitsev's story was relatable; he was just a poor shepherd's son. But even the poorest Russian could rise to greatness in the USSR in the struggle against fascism.

To make the story more personal and dramatic, the propaganda machine of the Soviet Union kicked into high gear and created the Major König story. No records in the well-kept German archives indicate there ever was a Major Erwin König—all of it was fiction. But why did Zaitsev insist it was true? There are three likely reasons. The first is the most likely. In Stalin's Soviet Union, when you were told to do something, you did it. Second, Zaitsev began to believe the story over time, which is a well-known phenomenon. Third, he enjoyed the fame and notoriety that came with it.

It doesn't really matter if the story isn't true. What is true is that Zaitsev and the other Soviet snipers made life a living hell for the Germans in Stalingrad. And these snipers weren't all male. During the war, 800,000 Soviet women fought in the front lines or in the air, and many of them were snipers. Some of them were very good and had higher kill totals than Vasily Zaitsev when the war ended.

Zaitsev died in 1991 at the age of seventy-six. He was buried on Mamayev Kurgan, along with Chuikov and many other heroes of the battle.

Illustration 14: Zaitsev's rifle in Stalingrad Battle Museum today

There is another interesting tale that seems to pop up. This story is about a young Soviet boy who was an apprentice shoemaker. There are various versions of It. You see one in *Enemy at the Gates*, there is another in the 1993 German film *Stalingrad*, and you can find more in literature. Either way, the story ends the same way. The young shoemaker, caught behind German lines, repairs the Nazis' boots. He observes them and listens in with his basic knowledge of German. He then feeds information back to the Russians, but he is eventually found out and hanged (or shot) by the Germans. There is probably some truth to the story somewhere.

Jumping back to the battle at hand, Stalingrad is also known for the battles that took place in the factories of the city. The three largest factories were the Stalingrad Tractor Factory, the Red October Factory, and the Barrikady Factory. Each of these factories, which were more like giant factory complexes than just one building, produced vital war supplies and did so during the battle unless they were captured. To capture them, the Germans brought in highly trained units of assault engineers from other fronts.

Fighting in the factory complexes was like a war within itself. At or near the Tractor Factory complex alone, an estimated 30,000 men died in three months. Think about that for a moment. In the *ten years* of the Vietnam War, the United States lost an estimated 58,000 men. With the casualties from all three factory buildings put together, it is likely 100,000 people lost their lives. Like the battles in the streets and buildings, these fights sometimes involved groups of Soviets on one side of a wall and Germans on the other.

Lastly, to supply the defenders of Stalingrad, the Soviets had only one choice: to bring in supplies and men from across the Volga, Europe's largest river. To do so, they had to run a gauntlet of German air and artillery attacks, which took a heavy toll. Boats that succeeded in making it to the city would bring out civilians, the wounded, and messages, among other things. They sometimes would not make it back to where they started, but as the battle went on, Soviet air defenses over the river grew in strength, making the voyage a bit safer before the river froze over in the dead of winter.

Chapter 6 – The Germans Get Beaten at Their Own Game

While the 6ᵗʰ Army was fighting in Stalingrad, the German drive in the Caucasus went on. The fighting there was hard, but it was not on the same level as Stalingrad. The Germans drove about halfway down the peninsula, sometimes fighting in beautiful Middle Eastern style cities laced with palm and orange trees, and at other times fighting in the unforgiving atmosphere of the snow-covered Caucasus Mountains. They never reached Baku and its rich oil fields. Although they did reach some of the smaller oil fields in the area, they found the equipment destroyed and the fields on fire. Even if the Germans had taken the area, it might have been months or even years before they could have made the area productive again.

By the end of December, the Nazis knew they were doomed if they stayed where they were, for the Soviets had turned the tables on Hitler in the area of Stalingrad.

On November 13ᵗʰ, 1942, Stalin approved Operation Uranus. In Russian myth and astrology, Aquarius was the ruling sign of Russia. The dominant planets of Aquarius were Uranus and Saturn, and it was from this that the Soviets named the operation they believed would inflict a mortal blow on the Germans at Stalingrad.

The planning for the Uranus counterattack had begun in September, at a time when things were looking very bad for the Red Army. But the STAVKA realized a number of things in their favor. Firstly, the German supply lines were seriously overstretched. The Russians knew how much supply was being destroyed or captured by the partisans on its way to Stalingrad.

Second, the German prisoners were in increasingly bad shape. These men had expected a quick victory and instead got a butcher's yard. As the fall went on and the weather got colder, the Soviets realized that their prisoners were getting thinner and sicker. One thing many people do not know about the Stalingrad campaign is that the Germans and their Hungarian, Romanian, and Italian allies suffered from an epidemic of tularemia. Tularemia is a rodent-borne disease native to the steppes of Southern Russia, Ukraine, and Central Asia. Most Soviet troops had been vaccinated for it, but the Germans didn't seem to know about it until it was too late. Tularemia attacks many areas of the body, including the lungs, lymph nodes, eyes, and skin. It can be fatal if not diagnosed and treated early. The disease, in addition to making one extremely uncomfortable (symptoms include itching, chills, and fever), also leads to massive headaches and exhaustion. The soldiers infected by tularemia often died.

Third, the Russians knew (as the Germans should have) that winter was coming. Even though it was their second winter of the war, the Germans were radically underprepared. However, the Soviets were ready. In the winter of 1942/43, temperatures reached -40°F. The illustration below, which was made before the end of WWI, shows an old Russian "ally," known to all as "General Winter."

Illustration 15: "General Winter" sweeps Russia's enemies before him

Fourth, the Soviets were aware of the deployment of Axis forces in the city and to the north and south of it. In Stalingrad itself, where the fighting was the most intense, one would see the Germans fighting. To the north and south, the Hungarians and Romanians (who often had to be kept apart by units of Italians and second-rate German troops because of the enmity between them) held the line. The troops of both of these countries had, at times, fought hard, especially at the outset of the war, when they seized lands in southern Russia and Ukraine, which were promised to them by Hitler. However, as the war ground on, their morale and willingness to fight decreased. On top of this, they were equipped with outdated weapons and had virtually no anti-tank weapons of any worth. Below, you can find images of Hungarian (top) and Romanian (bottom) soldiers.

Lastly, the Soviets knew that they had millions of more men in the training pipeline and in reserve, which was something the Germans just couldn't believe. One million of these men were detailed for the upcoming operation, a more strategic move than throwing them into the city one by one.

Operation Uranus was the product of much planning and much secrecy. Only two men, Stalin and the chief of staff of the Red Army, Marshal Boris Shaposhnikov, knew the entire plan. The commanders on the various fronts only knew the relevant parts of the plan. There were three main Soviet fronts: the "Stalingrad Front" to the south of the city, commanded by General Andrey Yeryomenko; the

"Southwest Front" to the north, commanded by General Nikolai Vatutin; and the "Don Front" within and facing Stalingrad, commanded by General Konstantin Rokossovsky.

For two weeks before the Soviet counteroffensive began, all mail flowing in and out of the area stopped. False radio traffic was set up, allowing the Germans to believe the Russians were almost at the end of their rope. Strict curfews, along with light and sound discipline, were enforced harshly. Most major movements went on only at night with dimmed lights, if any.

For weeks, the Soviets had been carrying out a careful balancing act in Stalingrad itself. They had been feeding just enough men into the city to keep the Germans busy and focused on their goal. All the while, they had been amassing troops on both sides of the ruined metropolis. Those of you familiar with the later career of boxing great Muhammad Ali will recognize this as a massive version of the "Rope-a-Dope," a move in which Ali would allow his opponent to tire himself out while reserving his own strength for the later rounds when he would deliver a knock-out blow, as with George Foreman in 1974.

Both attacking Soviet fronts had about half a million men. Almost 900 tanks were divided between them, as well as nearly 14,000 guns and 1,500 aircraft. Facing them were about 250,000 Germans (many of them within the city), perhaps 500 guns, 400 serviceable aircraft, and a couple hundred serviceable tanks of various types. Romanian, Hungarian, and Italian forces on the flanks numbered about 500,000 men, but both the German forces and their allies were suffering from hunger, poor morale, bad equipment (especially in the case of the allies), and poor supply. By contrast, Soviet morale was exceedingly high and about to get higher.

On the mornings of November 19th and 20th, the Soviet forces counterattacked in the north first. Then, after the Germans' attention had been shifted northward, the southern Soviet forces attacked. The weather was bleak throughout all of November. It was far below freezing, and a frozen mist hung above the battlefield, making visibility and hearing poor.

Soviet/Russian propaganda has carefully cultivated an image of hundreds of thousands of white-clad Soviet soldiers on racing T-34 tanks, emerging out of the mists to take the Germans and their allies by complete surprise and sowing terror far behind the front lines. In this case, the propaganda is pretty accurate. Adding to the Germans' fear was the launching of hundreds of thousands of Katyusha rockets, which were fired just ahead of the charging tanks. These weapons, called "Stalin's organ" by the Germans for the eerie sound they made, were not very accurate, but they could discharge hundreds of small artillery shell-sized rockets to saturate a small area, many times destroying everything in their path.

One of the Germans facing the Russians was Gunter Koschorrek, whose memoirs were published in 2011 as BLOOD RED SNOW: THE MEMOIRS OF A GERMAN SOLDIER ON THE EASTERN FRONT. He wrote, "Wilke yells, 'Tanks are coming! In great masses! Swarms of them!' His last words are drowned out by the noise of the explosions from the shells the tanks are firing at us. Then I see them too! First, it's like a wall of fire advancing on us, then a horde of brown beetles slowly approaches across the white steppe...So this is what the Soviets have prepared: a colossal tank attack."

Within hours, the German allies on the flanks, as well as the few German units there, either panicked and fled, were killed, or were taken as prisoners. The Soviet tankers were not hesitant to get their revenge. At times, they would drive on top of an enemy trench or foxhole and then hold one track still while driving the other track forward or backward. This had the effect of spinning the tank, which ground it into the dirt, crushing and grinding anyone unfortunate enough to be underneath. The retreating German troops running across the steppe were purposely run over by the hundreds. Both sides employed this terrifying tactic as the battle progressed.

The Soviets drove far deeper than the Germans could have ever imagined. They crossed the Don River at Kalach, some seventy or so miles from Stalingrad. On November 23rd, the two prongs of the Soviet attack came together in that area. The Germans and their allies in Stalingrad and its vicinity were surrounded, and the nearest German forces were some sixty to seventy miles away.

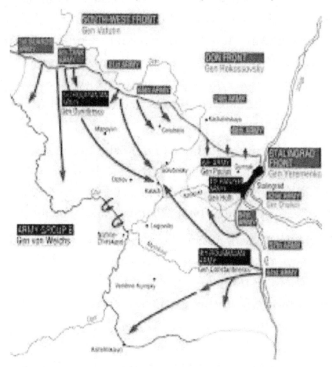

Illustration 16: Operation Uranus

When Hitler and the German High Command heard the news, they were incredulous. Where had all these men come from? Still, reports came flooding in about the scale of the setback. Almost right away, many of Hitler's generals, both in Germany and in the field, recommended that he order the forces in Stalingrad to attempt a breakout and have the German forces in the Don bend area attack toward them, which would open a gap in the Soviet forces for the remnants of the 6th Army to withdraw through. Hitler refused. Instead, he ordered Paulus to remain in place.

In Stalingrad, Paulus and his staff vacillated between thinking they could hold out until a relief force could be sent, thinking they could break out themselves, and feeling doomed. Of course, with each passing day, the feeling of doom increased.

When the scope of the Soviet counterattack became perfectly clear, Hitler ordered his forces in the Caucasus to withdraw—most of them were already doing so on their own. What was left of Hitler's forces in the Caucasus didn't cross over into Crimea until the spring of 1943. Even at that point, when all reality dictated otherwise, Hitler didn't allow his troops in Kerch to cross over to the Crimean Peninsula because he thought he needed a foothold there for when his troops returned to the area.

Stalingrad was when Hitler really began his descent into "unreality." Over and over again, he ordered his men to stay in the city, believing that his best general, Erich von Manstein, would break through the Russian lines and help Paulus retake the city.

The Germans argued among themselves until they began an attack on the southern area of the Soviet front, hoping to break through to the city. Paulus was ordered to stay in place. Though many historians have said the best option was for Paulus's forces to breakout to the south to meet Manstein, more recent analyses indicate that almost right from the start, Paulus's half-starved frozen men would have lost 50 percent of their strength. If Hitler had immediately ordered a relief force before the Soviets could dig into their new lines, Paulus might've had a chance. Operation Winter Storm (*Unternehmen Wintergewitter*), the German counterattack, which included 13 divisions (which were mostly under-strength), some 50,000 men, and 250 tanks (including the new "Tiger"), was pretty much doomed from the start. However, the focused nature of the operation and the experience of the German troops and commanders allowed them to penetrate some fifty to sixty miles. But that was about as far as they would go. After being surprised by the German effort, the Soviets reacted strongly, and they stopped the German relief effort in its tracks by December 13th. The offensive had only begun on the 11th.

The almost 250,000 German men inside the shrinking Stalingrad pocket were fighting for their lives. Almost every day, the pocket got smaller. Men were eating rats and slowly starving and freezing to death. After it was clear that the relief effort would fail, Paulus repeatedly asked Hitler for permission to surrender. Hitler refused every time. Finally, growing tired of Paulus's entreaties, Hitler promoted Paulus to the rank of field marshal, the highest rank in the German Army. The Führer knew that no German field marshal had ever surrendered. Instead, they would take their own life. That message was not lost on Paulus.

Hitler's air force chief, Hermann Göring, promised the Führer he would deliver the 300 tons of supplies needed for the men in Stalingrad daily. He never delivered more than 150 tons in one day. Most of the time, it was far less. Weather, Soviet planes, and anti-aircraft guns destroyed the rest.

Once the German planes landed, they would take out the wounded or those with "pull" in the Nazi Party. The scenes at the last German-controlled airfield when the last planes were leaving could not have been more pitiful. Guards at the doors shot into crowds of men as they attempted to force their way onto the planes. Some of the guards were pulled out of the planes and killed. Planes were overloaded and sometimes crashed. Others had men hanging off the wings, who then tumbled to their deaths while their comrades watched. Everyone in Stalingrad knew that being a Soviet prisoner was a virtual death sentence.

On January 22nd, 1943, Paulus gave the order for his men to surrender. A pocket of "die-hards" in the northern part of the city held out until February 3rd. Even after the surrender, German broadcasts at home featured interviews with men "on the front on the Volga," but these were recorded in Germany with combat sounds edited in. By the time most Germans heard them, Stalingrad had already been surrendered.

Ninety-one thousand Germans went into Soviet captivity. Ten years after the war ended in 1945, the last Germans in the USSR, numbering around 5,000, were sent home.

Illustration 17: Top: Paulus, on the left, and his staff upon surrender. You can see his HQ building in the background. Bottom: Picture of HQ building today.

Illustration 18: Germans surrendering at Stalingrad

Illustration 19: "The Motherland Calls" on Mamayev Kurgan. This is one of the tallest free-standing statues in the world at 279 feet.

Conclusion

Stalingrad was the "high-water mark" of the German Army in the USSR. After Stalingrad, the war, not only in Russia but everywhere, went decidedly against Hitler. There was only one time after the battle that the Germans were able to launch a major offensive in the East. This was at Kursk in July 1943. However, this, too, was a colossal defeat.

Stalingrad changed everything. Soviet morale soared through the roof, and Soviet strength increased, though they had sustained unreal casualties. The Soviets also began to master the "new" tactics of modern mobile warfare that had been introduced by the Germans in 1939. In actuality, while the Soviets became masters at mobile warfare and surprise, the Germans, guided by Hitler's stubborn refusal to give an inch of ground, reverted to digging in. This resulted in the Germans being isolated and cut off time and again, just as the Soviets had been in the first stages of the war.

Though many in Germany needed to believe the war could still be won, most knew something terrible had happened on the Volga. This was reinforced when survivors of the battle were evacuated before the end of Operation Uranus and the last airlifts. Already becoming a recluse, Hitler retreated further and further into his fantasy land, leaving much of the war effort to his propaganda chief, Joseph Goebbels. Goebbels began making speeches around the country, urging a greater effort from the German people. The slogan he touted was "Total War, Shorter War!" By this point, even the Nazis knew the Germans were getting tired of the war effort and the millions of casualties. And it all began at Stalingrad.

Here's another book by Captivating History that you might be interested in

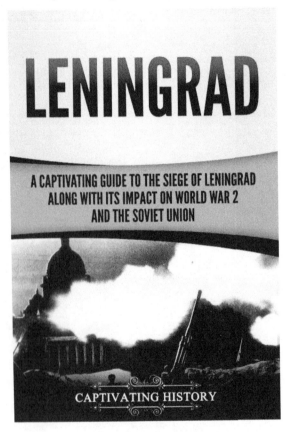

References

Beevor, Antony. STALINGRAD: THE FATEFUL SIEGE: 1942-1943. London: Penguin, 1999.

Busch, Reinhold. SURVIVORS OF STALINGRAD: EYEWITNESS ACCOUNTS FROM THE 6TH ARMY, 1942-43. Frontline Books, 2014.

Craig, William. ENEMY AT THE GATES: THE BATTLE FOR STALINGRAD. New York: Penguin, 1974. (Much better than the 2001 movie which was loosely based on it)

Dear, Ian, I. C. Dear, and M. R. Foot. OXFORD COMPANION TO WORLD WAR II. Oxford: OUP Oxford, 2001.

Koschorrek, Gunter. BLOOD RED SNOW: THE MEMOIRS OF A GERMAN SOLDIER ON THE EASTERN FRONT. Frontline Books, 2011.

Liedtke, Gregory. ENDURING THE WHIRLWIND: THE GERMAN ARMY AND THE RUSSO-GERMAN WAR 1941-1943. Helion and Company, 2016.

Merridale, Catherine. IVAN'S WAR: LIFE AND DEATH IN THE RED ARMY, 1939-1945. London: Macmillan, 2007.

Overy, R J. WHY THE ALLIES WON. New York: Random House, 2006.

SERVICE, ROBERT. STALIN: A BIOGRAPHY. Cambridge: Harvard University Press, 2005.

Movies/Programs about the Battle of Stalingrad, with author's recommendations:

Stalingrad: Dogs, Do You Want to Live Forever? (1959) - Drama, black and white, German language with subtitles. A bit slow but excellent.

Stalingrad (1993) - Drama, color, German language with subtitles. Somewhat of a remake of the above film but better and more balanced.

Soviet Storm: WW2 in the East (2011) - Documentary, Russian-made but balanced with historians from both sides. Moves well for a documentary.

World at War: Stalingrad (1973) - Documentary. Still holds up after 47 years, and how can you go wrong with Laurence Olivier narrating?

Enemy at the Gates (2001) - Based on the 1974 William Craig book, the movie is a dramatic retelling of the famous "sniper battle" involving famed Soviet sniper Vasily Zaitsev. Take it with a grain of salt, and you'll enjoy it immensely.

Made in the USA
Las Vegas, NV
06 March 2022

45162765R00049